Math = Fun!™

Weights
and
Measures

by Jerry Pallotta
Illustrated by Rob Bolster

SCHOLASTIC INC.

New York   Toronto   London   Auckland   Sydney
Mexico City   New Delhi   Hong Kong   Buenos Aires

For Dana Morrissey, the cutest NCDS girl!
—*J. P.*
To the Huckles!
—*Rob Bolster*

Text copyright © 2008 by Jerry Pallotta
Illustrations copyright © 2008 by Rob Bolster
All rights reserved. Published by Scholastic Inc.
SCHOLASTIC, MATH = FUN!, and associated logos
are trademarks of Scholastic Inc.

ISBN-13: 978-0-545-06448-4
ISBN-10: 0-545-06448-1

12 11 10 9 8 7 6 5 4 3 2   8 9 10 11 12 13/0

Printed in the U.S.A.
This edition first printing, September 2008

Welcome to weights and measures! Here are some words: foot, gallon, ounce, meter, mile, pint, quart, and many more. What do they all mean? Let's start reading and find out.

chicken's foot

elephant's foot

mouse's foot

baby's foot

basketball player's foot

If something is a foot long, how long is it? Is it as long as an elephant's foot? Is it as long as a chicken's foot, a baby's foot, a basketball player's foot? These feet are all different lengths.

ruler

Everyone needs to use the same measurement when describing a distance or a length. Here is a ruler. It will help us measure things.

inch 1

Here is one inch.
The green inchworm is showing us how long one inch is.

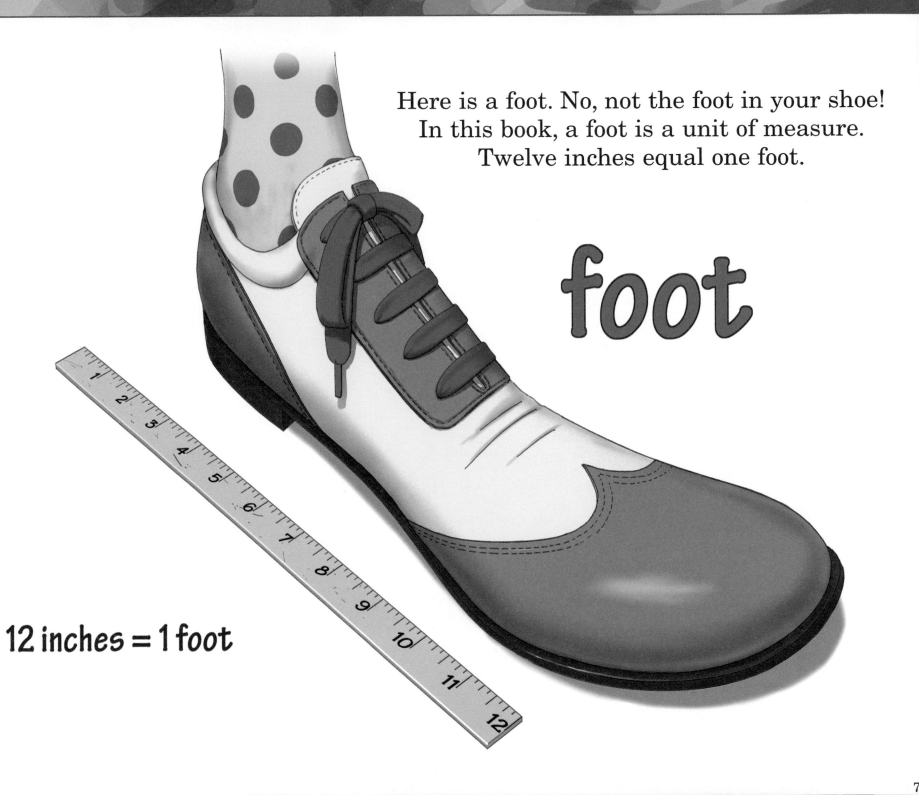

Here is a foot. No, not the foot in your shoe! In this book, a foot is a unit of measure. Twelve inches equal one foot.

foot

12 inches = 1 foot

yard

12 inches = 1 foot
3 feet = 1 yard
36 inches = 1 yard

If something is a yard long, it does not mean the same thing as the yard behind someone's house. One yard is the same length as three feet. Thirty-six inches is the same as one yard.

mile

1 mile = 1,760 yards
1 mile = 5,280 feet

finish

How long is a mile? It is exactly one thousand seven hundred sixty yards.
It is also five thousand two hundred eighty feet.
Maybe you should go out for a one-mile jog.

metric length measurements

In most countries outside the United States, people do not use inches, feet, yards, or miles. They have a different system of measurement. They use the metric system, which uses different units of measure. If you can count by tens, you can figure out the metric system.

10 centimeters

Here is a centimeter. A centimeter is the same length anywhere in the world. It is as wide as one of these colored squares.

decimeter

Ten centimeters is called a decimeter.

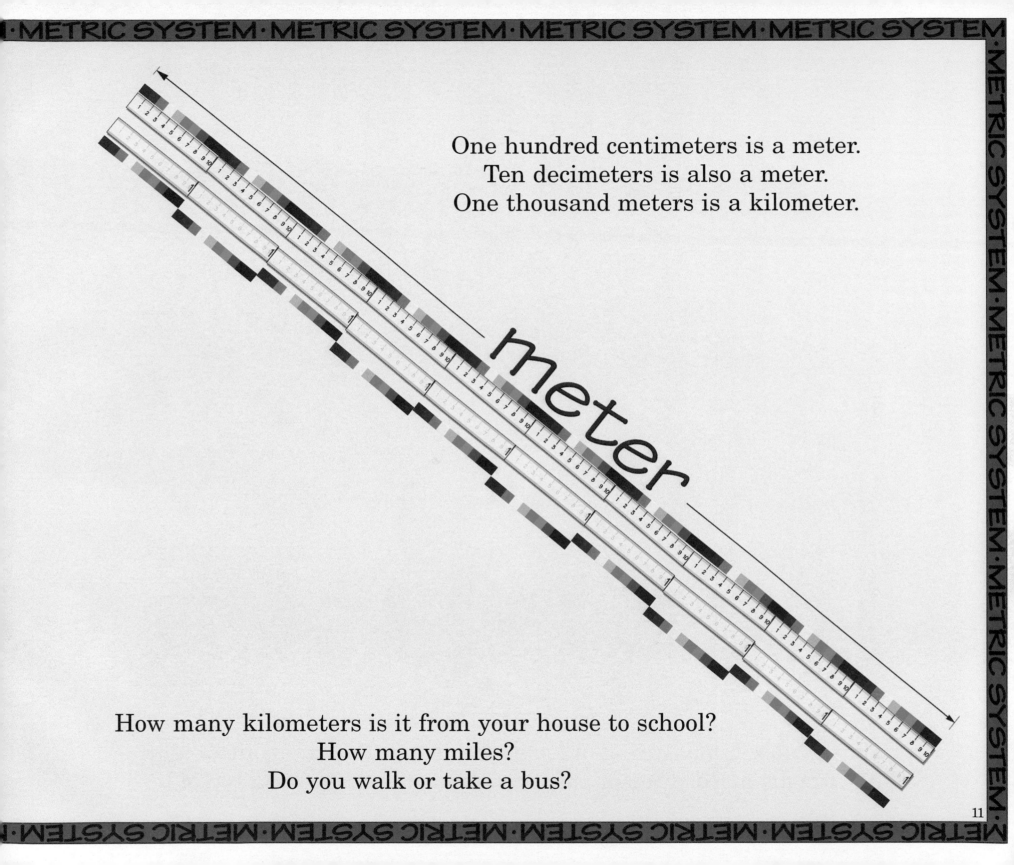

One hundred centimeters is a meter.
Ten decimeters is also a meter.
One thousand meters is a kilometer.

How many kilometers is it from your house to school?
How many miles?
Do you walk or take a bus?

That's enough measuring of length or distance! How about weight?
What weighs more: a ton of peanuts, a ton of feathers, or a ton of lead?

That question was a tricky one! An elephant would pick the peanuts.
Do not be fooled by size. These tons all weigh the same!
A ton is a standard measure.

ounce

Here is one ounce. It is a measure of a specific amount of weight. This cute little frog weighs one ounce and is probably in preschool. Five nickels and one penny also equal one ounce.

pound

A pound is sixteen ounces. If someone asks you, "How much do you weigh?"
it is very common to give the answer in pounds.
This frog weighs one pound and is probably in second grade.

five pounds

Wow! Here is a frog that weighs five pounds.
This frog is most likely in fifth grade.

ton

2000 pounds = 1 ton

A ton is two thousand pounds. This pile is a ton of green grapes.
Do not eat them all at once!

metric weight measurement

Remember the metric system?
The metric system also deals with weights.

Here is a small unit of weight: a milligram.

1,000 milligrams = 1 gram

gram

A thousand milligrams is called a gram. No, not "Gram" as in a nickname
for your grandma. A gram is a measure of weight.
The average almond weighs about one gram.

kilogram

1,000 almonds

1,000 grams = 1 kilogram

One thousand grams is a kilogram. One thousand kilograms is called a metric ton.
What weighs more, a ton or a metric ton?
The answer is hidden on this page.

What if you ask for some milk?
It is important to say how much you want. If you don't,
you might get a teaspoon, a tablespoon, or a teeny-weeny thimble full.

Or you might get a tanker truck full of milk.
Liquids need to be measured, too. When measuring liquids,
we do not use length or distance. We use volume.

fluid ounce

CHOCOLATE SYRUP

8 oz.

7 oz.

6 oz.

5 oz.

4 oz.

3 oz.

2 oz.

1 oz.

Here is one fluid ounce of chocolate syrup.
Let's make chocolate milk!

cup

In this book, a cup does not mean a glass or a cup from your kitchen cabinet.
One cup is eight fluid ounces.
Here is a cup of chocolate milk. Mmmm, delicious!

If you drink two cups of chocolate milk, it is the same as drinking a pint. Two cups equal one pint. A pint is also equal to sixteen ounces.

quart

2 pints = 1 quart
4 cups = 1 quart
1 quart = 32 ounces

Waiter, waiter, I would like to order one quart of chocolate milk, please.
Two pints equal one quart. Four cups equal one quart.

gallon

4 quarts = 1 gallon

8 pints = 1 gallon

16 cups = 1 gallon

Four quarts equal one gallon. One quart is a quarter of a gallon.
That's where the word "quart" comes from.
How many pints are in a gallon? How many cups?

billions of gallons

How many gallons of water are in the ocean?
Billions and billions and billions of gallons.
What if the ocean were made of chocolate milk?
The whales probably wouldn't like it.

metric liquid measurement

There is a metric system for liquids, too.
The system is based on the liter as the unit of measure.

 milliliter Here is one milliliter.

 = Ten milliliters equal a *centiliter*.

One hundred centiliters equal a liter.

Many different types of drinks are sold in one-liter bottles.

kiloliter

One thousand liters is called a kiloliter.
How many liters do you think it would take to fill this tub?

time

second

minute hour

60 seconds = 1 minute

60 minutes = 1 hour

24 hours = 1 day

There is another thing we measure.
It is called time! How long did it take to read this book?
Did it take a second, a minute, or an hour?

day week **year**

7 days = **1** week
52 weeks = **1** year
12 months = **1** year

There are twenty-four hours in one day. There are seven days in one week.
There are fifty-two weeks in one year. There are also twelve months in one year.
Did it take you one year to read this book?
There is no such thing as *metric time*.

Here is something we cannot measure.
We cannot measure how much you love reading.
We hope you always love to read!